中 計

A clever rabbit *has* three hiding places

CHAO-HSIU CHEN

A clever rabbit *has* three hiding places

STRATEGIES FOR SUCCESS IN LIFE

108 Stratagems from Ancient Chinese Wisdom

CONNECTIONS
BOOK PUBLISHING

A CONNECTIONS EDITION
This edition published in Great Britain in 2002 by
Connections Book Publishing Limited
St Chad's House, 148 King's Cross Road, London WC1X 9DH

This edition published in the U.S.A. in 2002 by
Connections Book Publishing Limited.
Distributed in the U.S.A. by Red Wheel/Weiser,
368 Congress Street, Boston, MA 02210

ISBN 1-85906-086-2

1 3 5 7 9 10 8 6 4 2

English translation by Doris and Robert Allen
Editorial: Nicola Hodgson, Liz Wheeler
Design: Hayley Cove
Production: Karyn Claridge, Charles James
Phototypeset in Bell MT using QuarkXPress on Apple Macintosh
Origination by Bright Arts, Singapore
Printed in Italy by Amadeus Industria Poligrafica Europea, Rome

CONTENTS

CONTENTS

CONTENTS

Introduction.

LIFE often resembles a battlefield – you must fight for what you desire. We all want to win but only a few are victors and even fewer can sustain their success. To win you do not need great force as long as you possess the secret of well thought-out strategy. It is this strategic ability that forms the art of fighting and the secret of winning.

The 5,000-year history of the Chinese empire was extremely turbulent. Political and military arguments, diplomatic intrigues, civil wars and revolutions resulted in sudden, violent changes of dynasty. This constant struggle for supremacy gave rise to great masters of ruse and deceit, men who could devise cunning strategies that would aid their emperors in gaining victory.

Many of these stratagems became so famous that they were handed down by tradition and eventually entered the language as proverbs. Their wisdom was applied not just to actual fighting but was found invaluable in dealing with all sorts of everyday situations. If you absorb this ancient Chinese knowledge it is possible, without spending much time, to find the best strategy for succeeding in all your undertakings. These stratagems do not only work when the situation is favourable to you, they are especially useful when fate appears to have turned against you.

The stratagems are taken mainly from ancient texts such as *Sun Tse Bin Fa* (Sun Tse's *The Art of War*), *Sanshiliu Gi* (*36 Stratagems*) and *Tai Gong Lio Tau* (Tai Gong's *Military Precepts*). Though they ostensibly relate to military matters, they are equally applicable to other situations and will help you to resolve arguments and doubts in work, business, love and daily life. Their wisdom helps to master even the most difficult situations.

There are many situations in which it is necessary to fight but, without the right strategy, success is uncertain. Strong muscles without a good brain do not guarantee success. A brain without muscles resembles a tree without roots, which will not be able to withstand either storms or rain. Even a magnificent brain without muscles is like a sapling whose roots need more time to grow in order to stand firm against storm and rain. However, the stratagems given here resemble tall trees with deep roots. Once you are familiar with them you can be sure of finding protection beneath their leaves and branches. Whenever you have to visit them, you can be certain of their assistance.

The stratagems are a pure life and survival philosophy, which can be used to help yourself and others, though it is important not to use their power to cause injury. Should you do so you will certainly end up being hurt yourself. In Chinese we say, 'Butterflies and bees never kill each other when fighting over the favours of the flower which serves them both. Rather, they both help it to propagate its beauty in the future.'

The first part of the book is divided into three sections, each of which has its own goal and contains thirty-six stratagems. Together they teach the art of subterfuge, which it is now possible for you to master. The first section explains how you can succeed in strengthening yourself for battle, the second tells you how to exploit your opponents' weaknesses, and in the third you will learn how to better yourself by turning difficult situations to your advantage.

The second part of the book looks at a wide variety of everyday situations you might meet in life, arranged alphabetically. Each situation appears as a heading with three statements and stratagems attached. When you are confronted with a difficulty and search for the answer, you will find guidance by looking under the appropriate heading in this part.

From the past we can learn to prepare for the future. Not only does the success of past masters gives us a standard to measure ourselves against, but also the mistakes of others can teach us vigilance. Nothing happens purely by chance. Behind everything there is a plan. If you can grasp the plan you are a master of your life, even if a bit of luck has to come into it. But even with luck you must find the right time, the right place and the right people to enable your plans to bear fruit. The stratagems will help you to recognize how to utilize your luck instead of letting opportunities pass you by. A master of life leaves nothing to chance and is always prepared. This is why a true master always belongs to the small group of victors.

I have added to the book thirty-six of my bamboo pictures and, to accompany each of them, I have written a motto which should encourage a deeper understanding of the stratagems. I chose the bamboo because it is regarded in Chinese art as the greatest symbol of strength and therefore stands for victory. The forces of nature may compel the bamboo to bend but it will never break and, before long, it once again stands up full of pride. Without doubt the bamboo is an accomplished fighter. His stratagem consists of only pretending to be beaten in order to come up again once the opponent has turned his back. The bamboo is clever, full of ruses and a master of life.

I

THE
THREE GREAT
GOALS

The following stratagems are divided into three sections each containing thirty-six entries. Each stratagem is accompanied by an interpretation that explains its deeper meaning. In the second part of the book you will find statements on everyday situations, each of which is accompanied by a stratagem. These will provide you with sound advice when faced with life's difficulties.

The First Goal

STRENGTHEN
YOURSELF

STRATAGEM 1

A good horse runs *by* itself

He who would be strong should free himself from all outside influences. He must avoid asking others for favours, for that would make him dependent upon them. Also he should let no one be in a position to exert influence over him and thus hinder his inner or outer development. He himself must determine the course of events. His independence will allow him to reach a free decision.

STRATAGEM 2

Hard polishing makes things shine

THE HUGE field of learning knows no frontiers and it takes deep study to attain your aims. He who makes great efforts and strives joyfully will one day succeed, even though he may suffer setbacks along the way. Some may succeed by doing nothing, but this will bring them no fame, and it is fame that makes the successful even more successful.

Open *your* eyes *to* make *the* clear view even sharper

EVERY detail, however insignificant it may appear, is important. Nothing is without meaning as all things are related to each other. That is why it is necessary to keep your eyes wide open at all times because only then can you truly appreciate what is really happening. Even little things deserve your respect, big ones demand your attention.

Use something worthless *to* attract something valuable

To UTTER empty words gives you a great advantage. Others will struggle to make better suggestions that put them in a good light. By refraining from sincere speech you will encourage others to utter wise words that you may use to your own advantage.

Never show *the* right what *is* being hidden *by the* left

IF YOU are badly prepared it is clever not to reveal your plans. Even when you are well prepared it is foolish to reveal everything. It is important to keep your options open so that you can react efficiently when the unexpected happens.

A clever rabbit *has* three hiding places

THE WORLD is full of hunters and each hunter brings danger. The hunted have their hiding places, but the hunter knows them too. That is why it is necessary to fool the hunter and offer him an empty hiding place while you have secretly prepared another place of safety.

Strive without rest to improve yourself.

The fox borrows *the* strength *of a* tiger

IF YOU have not got what it takes to achieve your aims, it is a good idea to stay close to powerful people. If you are clever you can borrow their power to advance your own ends.

Turn
from guest
to host

A GUEST is in a subordinate and dependent role, but a host is in charge of things. In order to change your role from guest to host you must give more invitations than you accept.

STRATAGEM 9

When *you* have reached *the* shore, sink *the* boat

In life you can look back but not go back.
When you have achieved something you may
celebrate but you must not stand still. In order
to develop yourself it is necessary at once to
undertake new endeavours. If you fail to develop
further you will lack aims, and to be without
aims is to be no longer fully alive.

Abandon gentleness *in* order *to* save *the* Emperor

SOMETIMES it is necessary to sacrifice something valuable in order to save something even more valuable. It may be hard to decide which is the more valuable and you may be unwilling to give up either. Even so, it is vital to make a quick, courageous decision.

Fish *for* trust *with* wounds

To GAIN someone's trust do not exhibit your strength but rather show vulnerability and by so doing attract help and pity. Self-inflicted wounds are useful to persuade others that you will make sacrifices for them. Of course, it is just as effective merely to pretend to be hurt.

Let *the* meal cook slowly

OFTEN it is better to delay your actions rather than let one deed follow another without any thought. Each action must be carefully considered before it becomes reality. Also, when the decisions of others have to be considered it is often better to postpone them skilfully, either because you feel that the time is not yet ripe, or because you feel that their actions would be to your disadvantage.

Enjoy the memory.

Fly like *a* dragon *with the* wind

PEOPLE often forget that they are a part of nature and that its power is incalculable. They think they can act without reference to nature, but they will learn better. It is always better to act in accordance with nature than to try to struggle against it foolishly.

Wear *the* most beautiful wig

When facing something great and mighty of which you are afraid, you have two main options. Either you remain as small and weak as you are and become prey, or you pretend to be as great and mighty as your opponent. Better still, pretend to be even more powerful. If you pull it off, your opponent will become your prey.

STRATAGEM 15

Make noise *in the* east *to* attack *in the* west

THROUGH the art of distraction you may often reach your goal. If the direct path does not lead to success, a ruse may be necessary. To distract your opponent you should kiss him on the left cheek so that you can slap him on the right.

With *a* light hand lead away *the* passing sheep

THERE are moments that only come once and you must always be prepared for them if you are not to miss your chance. Once you recognize such an opportunity it requires little effort to profit from it.

Steal *a* beam *and* replace *a* post *with* mouldy wood

To REPLACE good with bad may help you to reach your goal. People who are not in a position to recognize your intention will not notice what you are doing. To replace something beautiful with something ugly may lead to the same result. Deception is a good way of preventing others from foiling your plans.

Rest *while* the enemy tires himself

To TIRE your opponent is the best preparation for victory. But how do you tire him out? Always force him to take the first step and limit your own effort to reactions.

Do not destroy what you have gained.

Use silence
in order
to make noise

THIS tactic is useful to lull your opponent into a false sense of security. When he feels that there is nothing to fear because nothing is happening, the surprise attack follows. You can also distract him by pretending to be engaged in some quite different mission at the same time.

Cause distraction *by* staging *a* great drama

IF YOU know your weak points but are cunning enough not to show them in public, then it is useful to appear free from faults. Thus you may attain great success with very little effort.

Gold does not fear *the* fire

IF YOU admit your weaknesses and know where you are vulnerable, you will react appropriately to setbacks. You are aware that you must develop yourself in order to avoid any such mistakes in future.

The condition *of the* road *is* tested *with* a single stone

WHATEVER you undertake, your first concern is to ensure that your task has a firm foundation. Without stability nothing can be attained and all will be lost despite your enthusiasm. Hope alone rarely brings success.

Borrow *a* strange coat *in* order *to* make *a* new beginning

IF YOU are disappointed do not give up hope but look around for a new ally in whose name you can make a new beginning.

Let *a* water buffalo pull *the* plough

TO TURN your ideas into reality you need the right foundations. You must find people who will be useful to you during the work and will help you build your own power base. To include others in your plans is always useful.

Contentment is wealth.

STRATAGEM 25

On reaching *the* goal, say goodbye *to your* companions

ONCE you have reached your objective it is better to continue without those who helped you attain your goal. Why? Because your former companions know how you got there, what methods you used and what weaknesses you are concealing. They are in a position to make these things public. Also your companions will want a share in your success as it was, after all, with their aid that you reached fame and honour.

Repair *the* roof before *it* rains

THE I CHING, the famous 'Book of Changes', teaches, 'The wise man lives in peace, but does not forget danger. He enjoys life, but does not forget death. He cares for order, but does not forget disorder.' No one can predict disaster, but you can be prepared so that, when it strikes, you are able to limit the damage.

STRATAGEM 27

Offer food only *to* *the* hungry

A GOOD deed is useful only if the recipient is really needy. Only in such a case can you be sure of his true gratitude and the deed will therefore be justified.

Use
the goodwill
of the fire

AN OLD ruse consists of starting a fire in order to attract attention. Then you loot the houses of those who are trying to put the fire out. That is why it is important to be doubly attentive during a fire because danger may threaten from the back as well as the front.

STRATAGEM 29

Hunt
a sheep
like *a* tiger

WHEN you have your goal in front of your eyes
you should think only of this and not let yourself
be distracted by anything else. Distractions lead
to you losing sight of your aim.

When *it* rains examine *the* roof, do not search *for an* umbrella

THE MORE you know of the bad deeds of others, the bigger is the danger in which you find yourself. That is why you live more safely if you never become a witness or an accessory. But what if it is unavoidable? Then you should open the door to the truth and trust the protection of the stronger power.

Daring should be kept within limits.

To save *the* peach, let *the* plum rot

IF THERE is no possibility of winning, it is better
to give up something unimportant instead of
losing even more. To part with something trivial
is often of more use than trying to hang on to it.

Sleep *on* wooden planks *and* eat earthworms

BEFORE reaching your goal and leading a pleasant life it is necessary to have known deprivation. Only then will you understand how to appreciate the good life.

Breathe out *the* old, breathe in *the* new

IN ORDER to create new possibilities it is necessary to part from people and things who hamper your progress. You should also leave behind those who do not want to better themselves as well as those who do not want to support your new plans.

Run away when *you* have to

WHEN things are hopeless and you are in danger, do not be ashamed to flee. Even if you cannot escape, you should surrender in the hope that you might yet rescue your plan. Then wait for the right time to pursue your aims once more.

Trust
the
growing tree

NOBODY is born wise. No great plan is quickly
realized. Everything needs time in order to attain
fulfilment. If success does not arrive quickly,
the wise rejoice.

Regard
success *as a*
mosquito

SUCCESS makes people proud. They conveniently forget the past and neglect to continue educating themselves. This path leads to failure. Thus the wise do not pay homage to their own success.

He who knows human nature needs no protection.

The Second Goal

WEAKEN YOUR OPPONENT

Saddle *the* horses before *the* journey

WHENEVER you feel strong enough to attack a problem you should immediately start by visualizing the solution. The same applies when you feel that the right moment has come to do something you have always wanted to do. Even when you are well prepared it is necessary to take all factors into account. Only take the initiative when you are well prepared.

Beware, *the* walls have ears!

THERE is no secret which would not bring advantage to someone if only they knew of it. Thus something that you would like to hide may suddenly become a danger to you and result in you losing control of the situation. Therefore only pass secrets on when you can be completely sure that no stranger will get his hands on them later.

STRATAGEM 39

Hold words behind *your* teeth

ANYTHING you say might be turned against you or used to hurt others. Before you say anything you should consider whether it will be useful or damaging. Choose your words with care, either to strengthen your own position or to weaken your rival's.

Let *the* phoenix loose *in* order *to* follow *the* dragon

SOMETIMES it is better to miss out on something important to avoid giving up on your plans which, after all, are more valuable even though they may not yet have come to fruition. In order to reach a great goal you should not hanker after security, and you must also be willing to accept initial losses. Your eventual success will demonstrate the value of your sacrifices, even though you may have found them scary at the time.

Do not spoil *the* dogs

NOBODY understands the joy of winning better than the victor himself. But to enjoy your victory to the full you must share it with no one. Many of your followers will also want to taste the delights of winning. Never let them out of your sight and be careful to keep a strict limit on their power.

See *the* invisible trap

EVEN though you may be completely blameless,
clever opponents can make you look guilty. It is
easy to notice the trap when it is too late. By then
it is nearly impossible to prove your innocence.
How can you avoid becoming entangled?
Be wary, trust only in yourself and tell your
secrets to nobody.

Defence knows no frontiers.

STRATAGEM 43

Do not submit under torture

THERE is hardly anyone who does not try to influence others or force their ideas on them. There are many ways of doing this, some are direct and some indirect. By seeing through your adversary's wiles in the early stages you will be able to withstand physical, psychological and emotional pressure.

Mistrust *the* favourite

NEVER trust people who are the favourites of others. Such people, in order to hang on to their position, tell you what they think you want to hear. They hang out their flag to see which way the wind is blowing. They seek to gain approval by following the majority opinion.

To catch *your* quarry *you* must let *it* run

IT IS useful not to catch your prey right away. Study your victim and learn his habits. Only when you are fully prepared should you attack.

Defend
your actions

EVERY plan needs a good reason, but if you are
wise you will also have a good excuse ready.
An excuse need not be a lie, though it need not
be close to the truth either.

STRATAGEM 47

Do not hit
the grass *to*
frighten
the snakes

IF YOU want to reach your goal it is better to
develop the stages of your plan in secret.
The more others know of your plans, the more
likely it is that you will fail in the early stages.

Do not attack *your* opponent without respect

To AVOID a power struggle becoming inhuman it is wise to treat your opponent with respect. In this way you will not only avoid harsh accusations but also keep an honourable reputation.

Everything needs a reason.

Convince *the* Master *of his* own strength

A RULER is only as strong as his subordinates let him be. He must be made to feel that he is only in his position because his subordinates have lent him their power voluntarily. If he should use this power against those who support him, he will have to be pushed off the throne.

Stab *with* someone else's knife

It is always good to reach your goal without doing anything yourself.

Scold *the* goat because *the* milk *is* sour

IF YOU have made a mistake and want to avoid punishment, find someone else on to whom you can shift the blame.

Befriend *the* distant opponent *in* order *to* attack *the* one next door

IT IS sometimes good to forge an alliance with someone who seems to be out of the question as a possible ally. In this way you can confuse your opponent and muddle his tactics. This scheme will help you to counter your enemy's strength and it works all the better because your actions will seem so inexplicable.

Hide *the* dirty shoes

IF YOU have done something wrong and face punishment, you would be wise either to remove the evidence or use it to shift the blame on to someone else.

Hunt
the wind
to catch
the shadow

RUMOURS can do great damage to your opponent. He will be forced to explain and defend himself even though there is no real evidence against him. Using your words to stir the imagination of others will help you to attain your goal easily.

He who is ignorant of the opposition suffers damage.

Slaughter *the* chicken *to* frighten *the* monkey

SOMETIMES it is not even necessary to attack your opponent directly. A warning shot may be enough to make him surrender or abandon his plans.

Pour oil
on to
the fire

IF YOUR competitor makes a mistake do not
hesitate to draw everyone's attention to it.
With skill you can turn a minor error into
an inexcusable offence.

Harrass *the* adversary without *a* sword

YOU NEED not use physical force to defeat your rival. It is enough to undermine his mind and spirit in such a way that he loses control and acts without thought. In this way he will reveal weaknesses from which you may later profit.

How
to turn
a nought
into a one

IF SOMEONE sends his opponent a message, it will not be the whole truth. If another person carries on the same message, he will be unsure of its veracity. If, however, someone else comes along who vouches for the truth of the message, he will change his mind and believe it immediately.

Watch *from* safety *the* fire *on the* opposite shore

IF YOU see a battle from afar, wait to see who wins and what advantage you may gain from the situation.

Use
the envoys

IF YOUR competitor wants to get hold of your secrets, you might be able to extract information from his agents. Also, you can let slip hints of your plan which they will take back with them and which will confuse and weaken him.

Obedience follows the water.

Capture
the leader *in* order *to* get rid *of* *the* robbers

AN ENEMY will be easily defeated if you take the leader prisoner. In this way his troops will lose their morale and be quickly dispersed.

Lure *the* tiger down *from the* mountain

SOMEONE who fights on his home territory has the advantage of local knowledge and is hard to defeat. The clever opponent will therefore do all in his power to lure him from his stronghold in order to inflict a decisive defeat at another location.

Surprise *the* enemy *in* order *to* save *your* ally

IF YOU want to help an ally who is under attack, you must strike suddenly at your enemy's weakest point so that you distract him and force him to release his grip. This brief respite may be used to free your ally from his predicament.

Pick off
your enemies
one
at a time

You can only defeat a more powerful opponent
if you dispose of his comrades one by one.

Lure *the* bird into *the* cage

IF YOU want to carry out a plan that is beyond your strength you must recruit an ally who is also enthusiastic for the project. Make him an offer so tempting that he cannot refuse.

Never look *for a* bone *in an* egg

To CRITICIZE yourself brings advantages. Criticizing others is futile.

To win before the battle.

Steal *the* fuel *from* under *the* kettle

IF YOU can remove your enemy's vital force you will never need to fear him in future.

How *to*
reverse
a stratagem

WHEN you spot a stratagem being employed
by your opponent it is clever to pretend you
have seen nothing. Then you may use his own
tricks against him.

STRATAGEM 69

Point *at the* mulberry *and* criticize *the* acacia

IF SOMEONE commits an error it is better, in order to avoid arguments, not to blame him directly. Instead you should tell him a story that makes it clear you know the truth, but in which you only mention his fault obliquely. In this way he will be beholden to you.

Kill
two birds
with
one stone

IF YOU are observant enough you might spot a second goal that lies close to your main objective. If you are quick-witted enough you may be able to achieve both aims at once.

Let

the quarry

praise

the hunter

IF YOU recruit a member of the opposition and gain his support, this is a decisive victory. Once you have disrupted their internal unity they can no longer oppose you wholeheartedly.

Pass *the* gate *of* beauty undamaged

HE WHO uses beauty to help his plans along will never lack success, but he who is taken in by beauty and commits himself to a plan without assessing it coolly commits a grave error.

Hearing the silence amongst the noise.

The Third Goal

DEVELOP
YOURSELF

STRATAGEM 73

Reach *the* city *of the* emperor *from the* four celestial directions

IT IS foolish to give up a plan just because it encounters difficulties. It is better to try a new and untried path to gain eventual victory.

Listen *to* *the* nightingale *and the* rook

Do not simply stick to your own views but pay careful attention to the opinions of others. Useful ideas may come from unlikely sources.

Have *as* many drops *as the* rain

To win alone is nearly impossible. You must have the collaboration of like-minded people. Thus a new force will be born which can be opposed only with great difficulty.

The wisdom *of the* fool

To PLAY the fool is often a good idea because you can realise your objectives without people suspecting what you are about. As long as nobody takes you seriously you can watch others and profit from their mistakes.

Build *a* temple *in the* hearts *of the* people

IF YOU want the support of a group of friends you must be sure of the affection of each individual member. To gain access to people's hearts is a major advantage, and not to disappoint them is your highest goal.

Be like *the* sea *that* welcomes *the* rivers

THE MORE you open your heart, the more thanks will flow towards you and this will lead to great success. The more you pass on this success, the more hearts you will open.

Sort out urgent matters carefully.

Join forces

THE RIGHT connections make success possible. But to create the right connections in the first place requires the greatest effort.

Unity
is
strength

THOUGH you are surrounded by followers there is no guarantee that you will always be successful. You will only succeed if each member protects the others.

Erect
a statue
to a whore

IN ORDER to undertake something immoral or forbidden you should give your plan a great name so that the people will support it with joy.

Climb up
with
your lips

THERE are always ears eager to hear flattery and lips eager to speak flattery. If the former belong to someone in a high position, and the latter to someone who is in a lowly position, then very soon you can be sure there will be two people in a high position.

Praise *a* sheep's head *in* order *to* sell dog meat

THERE is no shortage of fools who let themselves be cheated and are even proud of the fact.

Play *in an* orchestra *on a* broken flute

IF YOU work with others but do not manage your task, when somebody notices it is a good idea to blame your materials.

Follow good advice, no matter who it comes from.

Hide
the dagger
behind
a smile

IT IS not a good idea to give away your true
intentions. Steady smiling leads to success.

Agree *from the* front, deny *from* behind

In order to proceed quickly with your plans it is sometimes necessary to become a member of a group with whose aims you must appear to be deeply in sympathy, even if you despise them in secret.

STRATAGEM 87

Sleep well *with* few pillows

It is better to pass only a few laws and make sure everybody obeys than many which are widely ignored.

Give
a drink
to the
thirsty

YOU NEED three things in order to win: the support of nature, the right moment, and the agreement of the majority. How is this to be achieved? By giving the people what they need to drink.

STRATAGEM 89

Leave
the net open
on one side

To KEEP yourself from harm it is better not
to deprive others of the opportunity of
self-development when pursuing your plans.
If they see that you do not want to rob them
of their liberty they will meet you with
respect and offer you their liberty with joy.

Make *the* assassin *your* brother

THERE is always someone who will be happy to do your dirty work for you. What will make him keen is not so much the offer of money but the feeling that he has become your brother.

War lives on deceit.

Learn *from* *the* teacher *and* *the* tinker

ALMOST everyone knows something worthwhile, and learning is the first step to success. That is why you should regard everyone as your teacher.

Lure *your* enemy *on to the* roof *and* pull away *the* ladder

To GET rid of an enemy it is only necessary to draw him into a situation from which there is no escape. Only then can you be completely sure of him.

Build
a fence *of*
wood
and
bamboo

ONE should not seek only to benefit from the strength of others. The wise man also studies their weaknesses so that he can correct his own faults.

Break
the
mould

IF YOU possess many gifts but keep them hidden, you will never be offered the chance to prove your worth and have the chance of being useful to others. That is why you must have the courage to grow in stature.

Winning equals the moon.

Do not let *the* cook work *as a* tailor

SUCCESS depends upon each partner taking responsibility for his own area. It is essential that everyone knows which part of the success each partner was responsible for, otherwise the whole enterprise will be put in jeopardy.

Do not let
the wolf
be a shepherd

You will only be a true leader if you are able to delegate the correct task to each person.

STRATAGEM 97

Force *the* bear
to seek
the lost honey

WHEN someone has made a mistake you would
do better not to punish the culprit immediately
but to ask him to find out for you who is to blame.

Cut off
the hair,
not
the plait

If you have done wrong and get found out,
it is good to repent very loudly. By so doing
you will win hearts and turn reproaches
into understanding.

Let *the* tiger become *a* lamb *and the* carp become *a* shark

IF YOU always meet people with goodness, they will soon take it for granted. On the other hand, if you meet them with strength, they will oppose you. That is why you should alternate goodness with strength. The gift of goodness is only recognized if it is given rarely. Likewise, people will only submit to your power if you do not use it habitually.

Join
the
choir

THE SECRET of lasting success is to get everyone to agree about their rights so that contentment develops. Nothing is more detrimental to success than people who do not live in harmony.

The spirit knows strength.

Brush *the* dust *from the* gown

In order to reach the top you must present yourself as being without inner or outer blemish.

Show *the* plums *in* order *to* forget *the* thirst

IF YOU want to lead others and get their support you have to promise them something they want. As soon as the goal has been reached you can break your promise, or keep it, or even do a bit of both. Cleverly applied, the promise of a reward will keep your followers keen.

Turn *into* a cockscomb *or* *an* ox's tail

IF YOU do not yet have the opportunity to be the leader of a big group it is enough for the moment to be the head of a small group or a subordinate member of a big group.

Whilst eating *a* grasshopper *the* praying mantis should keep *a* sharp lookout *for* birds

NEVER, but never, forget to keep looking over your shoulder even as you move resolutely forward.

Stratagem 105

Do not steal without rules

WHATEVER you do, it should not be allowed to happen without order. Whatever you want, you must do it by the rules.

Enter *the* hut three times

You MUST bend your head when entering the hut where an advisor lives. If he will not see you the first time, try again and again until you have bent so low that he will give you what you want.

Remain modest in victory.

Make
everyone
happy

THE HIGHEST art is to unite friend and foe so
that both believe they have gained an advantage.

Never mix wine *with* milk

To LIVE happily everyone should be in the place where he belongs. That is why it is wise to ensure that everyone is contented with his lot.

II

WAYS TO LIFE MASTERY

E ach of the following pages contains three statements on typical situations you might meet in life. Search for a passage that applies to you. When you have found it you will also see a reference to a stratagem from Part I of the book. If you turn to the appropriate stratagem you will find good advice that will help you overcome your difficulties and succeed in your aims.

Affairs

I want to finish an affair.

> Stratagem 94
> *Break the mould*

I want to hide my affair.

> Stratagem 19
> *Use silence in order to make noise*

I want to end the affair which is causing me problems.

> Stratagem 107
> *Make everyone happy*

Anger

I cannot control my temper.

> Stratagem 21
> *Gold does not fear the fire*

I know that someone is angry with me but is it wise to try to modify the rage of others?

> Stratagem 98
> *Cut off the hair, not the plait*

The rage that is unleashed against me is unjustified but no one believes me.

> Stratagem 58
> *How to turn a nought into a one*

WAYS TO LIFE MASTERY

ARGUMENTS

I ARGUE more and more often with my partner.

STRATAGEM 3

Open your eyes to make the clear view even sharper

I HAVE fallen out with my business associates.

STRATAGEM 10

Abandon gentleness in order to save the Emperor

THE ARGUMENTS with my child have escalated.

STRATAGEM 11

Fish for trust with wounds

Attack

I did not want to attack but I was forced to. Now
I have won the battle but lost most of my friends.

Stratagem 77

Build a temple in the hearts of the people

I do not know when the right time to begin my
attack is.

Stratagem 37

Saddle the horses before the journey

I want to cease hostilities but my opponent
continues to attack.

Stratagem 100

Join the choir

ATTENTION

I WANT people to pay me more attention.

STRATAGEM 11

Fish for trust with wounds

I WANT to give others more attention.

STRATAGEM 74

Listen to the nightingale and the rook

I WANT more attention from those I love most.

STRATAGEM 78

Be like the sea that welcomes the rivers

BANKRUPTCY

I AM bankrupt and want to start again.

> STRATAGEM 23
>
> *Borrow a strange coat in order to make*
> *a new beginning*

I AM bankrupt and now everyone avoids me.

> STRATAGEM 65
>
> *Lure the bird into the cage*

I AM bankrupt and do not know what to do next.

> STRATAGEM 24
>
> *Let a water buffalo pull the plough*

Reach our goal without effort.

BEAUTY

MY BEAUTY is fading.

STRATAGEM 13

Fly like a dragon with the wind

I AM trapped by beauty.

STRATAGEM 68

How to reverse a stratagem

MY BEAUTY causes arguments.

STRATAGEM 59

Watch from safety the fire on the opposite shore

BUSINESS

I WANT to go into a new business.

STRATAGEM 22

The condition of the road is tested with a single stone

I WANT to invest without losing any money.

STRATAGEM 24

Let a water buffalo pull the plough

I FEAR that my business will bring me harm.

STRATAGEM 40

Let the phoenix loose in order to follow the dragon

Business
PARTNERS

I am seeking the right business partner.

STRATAGEM 93
Build a fence of wood and bamboo

My business partner is becoming too powerful.

STRATAGEM 52
Befriend the distant opponent in order to attack the
one next door

I am being blackmailed by my business partner.

STRATAGEM 43
Do not submit under torture

CARE

ALL MY errors happened because I did not take enough care.

STRATAGEM 101

Brush the dust from the gown

I WAS too careful and have missed my chance.

STRATAGEM 70

Kill two birds with one stone

I AM careful but the others are too exuberant.

STRATAGEM 93

Build a fence of wood and bamboo

CHARACTER

MY CHARACTER makes it hard for me to handle defeat.

STRATAGEM 21
Gold does not fear the fire

MY PROBLEMS are caused by my character.

STRATAGEM 33
Breathe out the old, breathe in the new

MY CHARACTER is such that I would rather run away than apply myself to a task.

STRATAGEM 7
The fox borrows the strength of a tiger

Children

My children have broken off contact with me.

Stratagem 65
Lure the bird into the cage

My children never follow my lead.

Stratagem 100
Join the choir

My children do not need me any more.

Stratagem 11
Fish for trust with wounds

The greatest victory is won over yourself.

CLIENTELE

,

THE CUSTOMER is always right, though often he is insufferable.

STRATAGEM 69

Point at the mulberry and criticize the acacia

I HAVE a new business, but no customers.

STRATAGEM 65

Lure the bird into the cage

I CANNOT deliver on time but do not want to lose my clientele.

STRATAGEM 51

Scold the goat because the milk is sour

COLLEAGUES

MOST COLLEAGUES leave me after a while.

STRATAGEM 95

Do not let the cook work as a tailor

MY COLLEAGUES try to betray me.

STRATAGEM 55

Slaughter the chicken to frighten the monkey

I CANNOT find suitable colleagues.

STRATAGEM 102

Show the plums in order to forget the thirst

COMPETITION

My competitors are becoming too powerful and reduce my winnings.

Stratagem 67

Steal the fuel from under the kettle

I want to get rid of my competitors.

Stratagem 92

Lure your enemy on to the roof and pull away the ladder

I do not want to admit that competition is good for business.

Stratagem 41

Do not spoil the dogs

CONSCIENCE

I HAVE a bad conscience and want to feel better.

STRATAGEM 51

Scold the goat because the milk is sour

SOMEONE is trying to give me a bad conscience for no reason.

STRATAGEM 42

See the invisible trap

MY PARTNER should have a bad conscience but does not.

STRATAGEM 69

Point at the mulberry and criticize the acacia

DANGER

I WANT to avoid danger.

> STRATAGEM 26
> *Repair the roof before it rains*

I LOOK for an escape from danger.

> STRATAGEM 10
> *Abandon gentleness in order to save the Emperor*

I AM in acute danger.

> STRATAGEM 15
> *Make noise in the east to attack in the west*

DEATH

I WANT to overcome my fear of death.

> STRATAGEM 26
> *Repair the roof before it rains*

MY PARTNER has died.

> STRATAGEM 33
> *Breathe out the old, breathe in the new*

I HAVE received death threats.

> STRATAGEM 102
> *Show the plums in order to forget the thirst*

Never climb a mountain without a companion.

DECEIT

MY FRIENDS deceive me time after time.

STRATAGEM 68

How to reverse a stratagem

MY BUSINESS partners are trying to cheat me.

STRATAGEM 67

Steal the fuel from under the kettle

I HAVE cheated someone and been found out.

STRATAGEM 53

Hide the dirty shoes

Defence

I NEED to defend myself against my enemies.

STRATAGEM 80

Unity is strength

I MUST defend myself against false accusations.

STRATAGEM 42

See the invisible trap

I NEED to defend myself against an over-mighty enemy.

STRATAGEM 64

Pick off your enemies one at a time

DEPENDENCE

I WANT to remove that which causes me harm,
but I am unable to do so.

STRATAGEM 32

Sleep on wooden planks and eat earthworms

I HAVE left my family, but I cannot manage alone.

STRATAGEM 75

Have as many drops as the rain

I FEEL under pressure from my colleagues,
but I cannot manage without them.

STRATAGEM 1

A good horse runs by itself

DIPLOMACY

WITHOUT diplomacy I cannot reach my goal.

STRATAGEM 85

Hide the dagger behind a smile

I WANT to say what I think even if it is undiplomatic.

STRATAGEM 39

Hold words behind your teeth

I AM aware that someone is behaving towards me in a diplomatic way but hides their true intentions.

STRATAGEM 68

How to reverse a stratagem

DISAPPOINTMENT

I HAVE experienced disappointment in love.

STRATAGEM 9

When you have reached the shore, sink the boat

I HAVE experienced disappointment in my professional life.

STRATAGEM 23

Borrow a strange coat in order to make a new beginning

I AM disappointed by life.

STRATAGEM 35

Trust the growing tree

DIVORCE

I DO not know whether I should get divorced.

STRATAGEM 5
Never show the right what is being hidden by the left

I DO not want to divorce because of the children.

STRATAGEM 63
Surprise the enemy in order to save your ally

I WANT a divorce but my spouse will not agree.

STRATAGEM 92
*Lure your enemy on to the roof and pull away
the ladder*

Dig a well before you are thirsty.

Doubt

I cannot get rid of my doubt.

Stratagem 32

Sleep on wooden planks and eat earthworms

I am doubted without reason.

Stratagem 94

Break the mould

Only my doubt drives me on.

Stratagem 36

Regard success as a mosquito

DUTY

I AM accused of having no sense of duty.

STRATAGEM 51
Scold the goat because the milk is sour

MY SENSE of duty causes me to suffer.

STRATAGEM 21
Gold does not fear the fire

I WANT to be free at last to do what I want.

STRATAGEM 90
Make the assassin your brother

WAYS TO LIFE MASTERY

ENEMIES

I WANT to dispose of my enemies.

STRATAGEM 92
Lure your enemy on to the roof and pull away
the ladder

I SEEK the right moment to attack my enemies.

STRATAGEM 37
Saddle the horses before the journey

I WANT to turn my enemies into friends.

STRATAGEM 89
Leave the net open on one side

ENVY

I AM sick with envy.

STRATAGEM 21
Gold does not fear the fire

I AM envied for my possessions.

STRATAGEM 6
A clever rabbit has three hiding places

I ENVY my best friend or partner.

STRATAGEM 103
Turn into a cockscomb or an ox's tail

Failure

I have no success in business.

Stratagem 10

Abandon gentleness in order to save the Emperor

I have no success in love.

Stratagem 29

Hunt a sheep like a tiger

My whole life is a failure.

Stratagem 29

Hunt a sheep like a tiger

FAME

I WANT to be famous.

STRATAGEM 101
Brush the dust from the gown

MY FAME is causing me suffering.

STRATAGEM 10
Abandon gentleness in order to save the Emperor

I AM afraid of becoming famous.

STRATAGEM 12
Let the meal cook slowly

Be prepared!

FATE

FATE has dealt me a heavy blow.

> STRATAGEM 10
>
> *Abandon gentleness in order to save the Emperor*

FATE has struck a heavy blow at my family.

> STRATAGEM 32
>
> *Sleep on wooden planks and eat earthworms*

I WANT to escape my fate.

> STRATAGEM 26
>
> *Repair the roof before it rains*

FEAR

I AM afraid of old age.

STRATAGEM 21
Gold does not fear the fire

I AM afraid of death.

STRATAGEM 9
When you have reached the shore, sink the boat

I AM afraid of loneliness.

STRATAGEM 8
Turn from guest to host

Fidelity

My partner is unfaithful.

STRATAGEM 45
To catch your quarry you must let it run

I want to be faithful but do not manage it.

STRATAGEM 66
Never look for a bone in an egg

My liberty is more important than fidelity.

STRATAGEM 10
Abandon gentleness in order to save the Emperor

FORCE

I CANNOT stand the pressure any longer, it is getting too much.

STRATAGEM 34

Run away when you have to

I AM being forced to do something against my will.

STRATAGEM 19

Use silence in order to make noise

I AM forcing myself to appear different from the real me.

STRATAGEM 20

Cause distraction by staging a great drama

Forgiveness

I cannot forgive others.

> Stratagem 20
>
> *Cause distraction by staging a great drama*

I cannot forgive myself.

> Stratagem 21
>
> *Gold does not fear the fire*

I have repented yet am not forgiven.

> Stratagem 53
>
> *Hide the dirty shoes*

FRIENDS

I WANT to have many friends from whom I can benefit.

STRATAGEM 84

Play in an orchestra on a broken flute

I WANT to rid myself of a so-called friend as quickly as possible.

STRATAGEM 56

Pour oil on to the fire

I AM not sure whether this friendship is selfless.

STRATAGEM 104

Whilst eating a grasshopper the praying mantis should keep a sharp lookout for birds

Success breeds success.

FUTURE

I AM frightened what the future will bring.

STRATAGEM 6

A clever rabbit has three hiding places

I KNOW that I am unable to offer my family a good future.

STRATAGEM 24

Let a water buffalo pull the plough

MY RELATIONSHIP has no future.

STRATAGEM 34

Run away when you have to

GOSSIP

I HATE gossip but have to indulge in it in order to gain an advantage.

STRATAGEM 86

Agree from the front, deny from behind

I AM the victim of gossip.

STRATAGEM 1

A good horse runs by itself

I WANT to avoid becoming the victim of gossip.

STRATAGEM 75

Have as many drops as the rain

GRATITUDE

ALTHOUGH I have helped others again and
again, they show me little gratitude.

STRATAGEM 27

Offer food only to the hungry

I WANT to make use of the gratitude shown
to me.

STRATAGEM 90

Make the assassin your brother

I WANT to inspire my children to show more
gratitude.

STRATAGEM 69

Point at the mulberry and criticize the acacia

GREED

I AM unjustly accused of greed.

STRATAGEM 33
Breathe out the old, breathe in the new

I WANT to benefit from my business partner's avarice.

STRATAGEM 83
Praise a sheep's head in order to sell dog meat

MY GREED will soon ruin a business relationship.

STRATAGEM 20
Cause distraction by staging a great drama

Guests

I want to get rid of a guest who has overstayed their welcome.

STRATAGEM 47

Do not hit the grass to frighten the snakes

My guest has offended me.

STRATAGEM 48

Do not attack your opponent without respect

I want to win over my guest and involve him in my plans.

STRATAGEM 90

Make the assassin your brother

GUIDANCE

I AM in need of guidance.

STRATAGEM 77

Build a temple in the hearts of the people

I WANT to stay in command.

STRATAGEM 95

Do not let the cook work as a tailor

I WANT to use guidance for the benefit of all.

STRATAGEM 96

Do not let the wolf be a shepherd

Pride will be punished.

GUILT

I HAVE made a mistake, but owning up would cause me problems.

STRATAGEM 51
Scold the goat because the milk is sour

SOMEONE wants to denounce me though I am innocent.

STRATAGEM 42
See the invisible trap

I AM not guilty but cannot prove it.

STRATAGEM 58
How to turn a nought into a one

HEALTH

ATTAINING my goals damages my health.

STRATAGEM 34
Run away when you have to

I HAVE to hide my poor health because of my career.

STRATAGEM 20
Cause distraction by staging a great drama

SOMEONE wants to damage my health.

STRATAGEM 68
How to reverse a stratagem

HONOUR

MY HONOUR is affronted.

STRATAGEM 57

Harrass the adversary without a sword

I WANT to be regarded as an honourable person.

STRATAGEM 101

Brush the dust from the gown

MY INTERESTS are in conflict with my honour.

STRATAGEM 17

Steal a beam and replace a post with mouldy wood

Hosts

I HAVE to invite someone I do not like but who might be useful to me.

STRATAGEM 82

Climb up with your lips

MY GUESTS ignore me.

STRATAGEM 65

Lure the bird into the cage

I AM invited and can make use of the host.

STRATAGEM 68

How to reverse a stratagem

HYPOCRISY

I HAVE discovered that someone is behaving hypocritically towards me.

STRATAGEM 68

How to reverse a stratagem

TO GAIN advantage I must, with reluctance, behave hypocritically.

STRATAGEM 82

Climb up with your lips

I WANT to avoid hypocrisy in the future.

STRATAGEM 21

Gold does not fear the fire

Independence

I want to be independent at last.

STRATAGEM 9
When you have reached the shore, sink the boat

I am looking for the right moment to become self-sufficient.

STRATAGEM 22
The condition of the road is tested with a single stone

I want to work in a team but remain independent at the same time.

STRATAGEM 31
To save the peach, let the plum rot

Never act without reason.

INFORMATION

I DO not know how to obtain the right information.

STRATAGEM 60
Use the envoys

I FEAR that my information might fall into the wrong hands.

STRATAGEM 38
Beware, the walls have ears!

I DO not know whether it is best to keep certain information to myself.

STRATAGEM 47
Do not hit the grass to frighten the snakes

INVESTMENT

I WANT to find the best opportunity to invest in.

STRATAGEM 74

Listen to the nightingale and the rook

I WANT to persuade others to invest in a business venture with me.

STRATAGEM 72

Pass the gate of beauty undamaged

I HAVE invested unwisely.

STRATAGEM 23

Borrow a strange coat in order to make
a new beginning

JEALOUSY

I SUFFER from jealousy.

STRATAGEM 21

Gold does not fear the fire

I WANT to hide my jealousy from my partner.

STRATAGEM 76

The wisdom of the fool

I AM jealous of my children's partners.

STRATAGEM 78

Be like the sea that welcomes the rivers

JUSTICE I

I HAVE done something good but am being treated badly for it.

STRATAGEM 68

How to reverse a stratagem

I HAVE to treat someone unjustly although I know that they do not deserve it.

STRATAGEM 50

Stab with someone else's knife

I HAVE done something unjust and have been caught out.

STRATAGEM 53

Hide the dirty shoes

JUSTICE II

WHATEVER I say I cannot get justice.

STRATAGEM 11

Fish for trust with wounds

MY PARTNER always wants to be right.

STRATAGEM 19

Use silence in order to make noise

I AM in the right but no one believes me.

STRATAGEM 58

How to turn a nought into a one

WAYS TO LIFE MASTERY

LANDLORDS

My LANDLORD has given me notice.

STRATAGEM 49
Convince the Master of his own strength

My LANDLORD makes more and more demands on me.

STRATAGEM 48
Do not attack your opponent without respect

I AM united with the other tenants against my landlord.

STRATAGEM 105
Do not steal without rules

The imperfect does not damage the perfect.

LIES

I AM being lied to and do not know whether
I should try to clarify the situation.

> STRATAGEM 76
> *The wisdom of the fool*

I HAD to tell a white lie.

> STRATAGEM 53
> *Hide the dirty shoes*

I KNOW that my whole life is one great lie.

> STRATAGEM 25
> *On reaching the goal, say goodbye to your companions*

LODGERS

I DO not want arguments with the lodgers
in my house.

STRATAGEM 87

Sleep well with few pillows

MY LODGERS have united against me.

STRATAGEM 61

Capture the leader in order to get rid of the robbers

MY LODGERS are making more and more
demands.

STRATAGEM 12

Let the meal cook slowly

LOSS

I HAVE suffered a big financial loss.

STRATAGEM 6

A clever rabbit has three hiding places

I WANT to turn my loss into gain.

STRATAGEM 88

Give a drink to the thirsty

ALL MY life I have been a complete loser.

STRATAGEM 20

Cause distraction by staging a great drama

LOVE

MY BUSINESS partner has fallen in love with me.

STRATAGEM 79

Join forces

I WANT to use love to gain success.

STRATAGEM 82

Climb up with your lips

THEY pretend to love me in order to further their ambition.

STRATAGEM 68

How to reverse a stratagem

Manipulation

I realize that I have been manipulated.

Stratagem 1

A good horse runs by itself

My attempts at manipulation have been discovered.

Stratagem 51

Scold the goat because the milk is sour

I am being forced to become manipulative.

Stratagem 68

How to reverse a stratagem

MARKETING

MY BUSINESS needs new marketing.

STRATAGEM 33

Breathe out the old, breathe in the new

I DO not know when the time is right to try
a new marketing strategy.

STRATAGEM 22

The condition of the road is tested with a single stone

MY COMPETITOR imitates my marketing.

STRATAGEM 52

*Befriend the distant opponent in order to attack
the one next door*

Do not torture the suspect.

MISFORTUNE

MY MISFORTUNE is the result of my failure.

STRATAGEM 21

Gold does not fear the fire

NOBODY helps me in my misfortune.

STRATAGEM 106

Enter the hut three times

SOMEBODY has made me unhappy.

STRATAGEM 97

Force the bear to seek the lost honey

MISTAKES

A FAMILY member has made an error.

STRATAGEM 69

Point at the mulberry and criticize the acacia

I HAVE made a mistake at work.

STRATAGEM 51

Scold the goat because the milk is sour

I AM accused of someone else's mistake.

STRATAGEM 42

See the invisible trap

MOBBING

I AM being mobbed.

STRATAGEM 37

Saddle the horses before the journey

I BELONG to a group who use mob tactics
without my knowledge.

STRATAGEM 42

See the invisible trap

I WANT to help someone who is being mobbed.

STRATAGEM 63

Surprise the enemy in order to save your ally

MONEY

SOMEONE tries to buy my support.

STRATAGEM 70

Kill two birds with one stone

I WOULD like more money but, with my job, it is not possible.

STRATAGEM 24

Let a water buffalo pull the plough

I JUST cannot manage money.

STRATAGEM 32

Sleep on wooden planks and eat earthworms

NEIGHBOURS

I AM constantly at loggerheads with my neighbours.

STRATAGEM 48

Do not attack your opponent without respect

I AM opposed to the close friendship my neighbour seeks.

STRATAGEM 31

To save the peach, let the plum rot

MY NEIGHBOUR conspires against me.

STRATAGEM 52

Befriend the distant opponent in order to attack the one next door

OBEDIENCE

I ALWAYS have to obey a member of the family.

STRATAGEM 49

Convince the Master of his own strength

MY CHILDREN do not want to follow my suggestions.

STRATAGEM 65

Lure the bird into the cage

MY EMPLOYEES do not follow my instructions correctly and believe I would not admit it.

STRATAGEM 55

Slaughter the chicken to frighten the monkey

A lie lives in the truth.

OLD AGE

I HAVE been given the sack because of my age.

STRATAGEM 9

When you have reached the shore, sink the boat

I HAVE lost my looks and my vigour.

STRATAGEM 103

Turn into a cockscomb or an ox's tail

I AM often over-critical of young people because,
unlike them, I have little left to expect from life.

STRATAGEM 108

Never mix wine with milk

Order

I AM criticized for being untidy.

STRATAGEM 20

Cause distraction by staging a great drama

I AM too tidy.

STRATAGEM 94

Break the mould

I AM suffering from the untidiness of my partner.

STRATAGEM 93

Build a fence of wood and bamboo

PARENTS

MY PARENTS do not want to understand me.

STRATAGEM 14
Wear the most beautiful wig

MY PARENTS expect me to fulfil their wishes.

STRATAGEM 43
Do not submit under torture

I CANNOT make myself understood in front
of my parents.

STRATAGEM 4
Use something worthless to attract something valuable

Patience

My children think I do not have enough patience with them.

Stratagem 12
Let the meal cook slowly

My partner complains that I do not show enough patience.

Stratagem 20
Cause distraction by staging a great drama

I have no patience at work.

Stratagem 21
Gold does not fear the fire

PERSEVERANCE

I FIND it hard to handle the tasks assigned to me.

STRATAGEM 2

Hard polishing makes things shine

FOR YEARS I have been trying to realize my schemes but without success.

STRATAGEM 24

Let a water buffalo pull the plough

I GET scolded because I do not have the patience and rigour to persevere.

STRATAGEM 20

Cause distraction by staging a great drama

POSSESSIONS

I HAVE many possessions but I am not happy.

STRATAGEM 45

To catch your quarry you must let it run

WHENEVER I gain some new possession I end up being disappointed.

STRATAGEM 40

Let the phoenix loose in order to follow the dragon

I WOULD rather be free of possessions.

STRATAGEM 33

Breathe out the old, breathe in the new

Justice has a long arm.

PRIDE

I FINALLY want to be proud of myself.

> STRATAGEM 94
> *Break the mould*

MY PRIDE has been hurt.

> STRATAGEM 91
> *Learn from the teacher and the tinker*

I NO longer have any reason to be proud
of myself.

> STRATAGEM 98
> *Cut off the hair, not the plait*

PRINCIPLES

I AM being forced to abandon my principles.

STRATAGEM 19

Use silence in order to make noise

I AM no longer sure of my principles.

STRATAGEM 22

The condition of the road is tested with a single stone

BECAUSE of my principles I have no more advantages.

STRATAGEM 31

To save the peach, let the plum rot

Profession

Many of those around me envy my position.

STRATAGEM 101
Brush the dust from the gown

I wonder whether my profession is really right for me.

STRATAGEM 22
The condition of the road is tested with a single stone

I do not know whether I should use my profession to pursue my interests or to make money.

STRATAGEM 10
Abandon gentleness in order to save the Emperor

PROMISES

I MADE a promise knowing that I cannot deliver.

STRATAGEM 102

Show the plums in order to forget the thirst

A PROMISE was made to me but I know that it will not be kept.

STRATAGEM 65

Lure the bird into the cage

I MADE a promise unwillingly but now I am being forced to keep it.

STRATAGEM 89

Leave the net open on one side

RELATIONS

I DO not get on with my relations.

> STRATAGEM 100
> *Join the choir*

MY RELATIONS bathe in my reflected glory.

> STRATAGEM 89
> *Leave the net open on one side*

MY RELATIONS are much richer than me.

> STRATAGEM 79
> *Join forces*

Relationships

I want to improve family relationships.

Stratagem 87

Sleep well with few pillows

I want to improve relationships within my firm.

Stratagem 99

Let the tiger become a lamb and the carp become a shark

I want to improve relationships within my business environment.

Stratagem 108

Never mix wine with milk

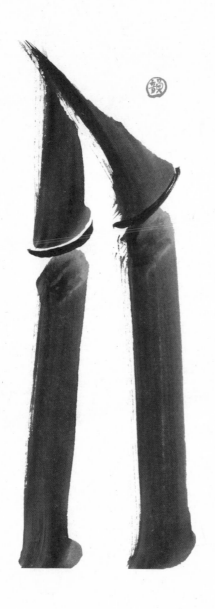

Friendship helps overcome errors.

Repentance

I REPENT a deed but I cannot undo the harm.

STRATAGEM 51

Scold the goat because the milk is sour

I DO not repent, even though some want to force me to.

STRATAGEM 98

Cut off the hair not the plait

I DO not know whether I will repent if I trust those with whom I find myself compatible.

STRATAGEM 44

Mistrust the favourite

REVENGE

I FEAR the vengeance of others.

STRATAGEM 6
A clever rabbit has three hiding places

I AM not sure whether I should take revenge.

STRATAGEM 40
Let the phoenix loose in order to follow the dragon

I WANT to take revenge on someone.

STRATAGEM 62
Lure the tiger down from the mountain

Rivalry

I know that my rivals are stronger than me.

Stratagem 64

Pick off your enemies one at a time

A rival is showing signs of weakness.

Stratagem 16

With a light hand lead away the passing sheep

I want to remain the best.

Stratagem 37

Saddle the horses before the journey

Rumours

I want to oppose an over-mighty opponent without effort.

Stratagem 54

Hunt the wind to catch the shadow

I want to convince someone of my intentions.

Stratagem 58

How to turn a nought into a one

I want to take advantage of a rumour.

Stratagem 71

Let the quarry praise the hunter

Savings

I WANT to use the savings of others.

> STRATAGEM 81
> *Erect a statue to a whore*

I WANT to invest all of my savings.

> STRATAGEM 24
> *Let a water buffalo pull the plough*

I HAVE lost all my savings.

> STRATAGEM 23
> *Borrow a strange coat in order to make*
> *a new beginning*

SECRETS

I CANNOT keep a secret.

STRATAGEM 20

Cause distraction by staging a great drama

I AM involved in secrets against my will.

STRATAGEM 30

When it rains examine the roof, do not search for an umbrella

SOMEONE is trying to extract a secret from me.

STRATAGEM 60

Use the envoys

Beautiful words are like a beautiful dress.

SECURITY

I ALWAYS seek the safest way, but that attracts criticism.

STRATAGEM 20

Cause distraction by staging a great drama

I AM offered security, but I do not know whether I should exchange it for my freedom.

STRATAGEM 22

The condition of the road is tested with a single stone

I AM paralysed by insecurity.

STRATAGEM 73

Reach the city of the emperor from the four celestial directions

SELFISHNESS

I AM not selfish enough.

STRATAGEM 21

Gold does not fear the fire

MY PARTNER is utterly selfish.

STRATAGEM 48

Do not attack your opponent without respect

MY GOAL is to overcome selfishness.

Stratagem 9

When you have reached the shore, sink the boat

SEPARATION

I SUFFER because of a separation.

STRATAGEM 21

Gold does not fear the fire

I WANT to avoid a separation.

STRATAGEM 5

Never show the right what is being hidden by the left

I WANT to bring about a separation as quickly
as possible.

STRATAGEM 46

Defend your actions

SHAME

I AM ashamed of my appearance.

> STRATAGEM 103
> *Turn into a cockscomb or an ox's tail*

I AM ashamed of what I have done but there is no turning back.

> STRATAGEM 53
> *Hide the dirty shoes*

I AM ashamed on behalf of someone else.

> STRATAGEM 69
> *Point at the mulberry and criticize the acacia*

Silence

I have discovered a secret but do not know whether to keep it or not.

Stratagem 76
The wisdom of the fool

If i speak up I can help someone, but doing so might harm me.

Stratagem 46
Defend your actions

Someone is forcing me to remain silent.

Stratagem 43
Do not submit under torture

SPOUSES

MY SPOUSE only does what he or she wants.

STRATAGEM 89
Leave the net open on one side

MY SPOUSE takes on no responsibility.

STRATAGEM 99
Let the tiger become a lamb and the carp become a shark

MY SPOUSE shows no patience.

STRATAGEM 50
Stab with someone else's knife

No knife remains sharp.

Struggle

I know that my opponent is stronger than me.

> Stratagem 18
>
> *Rest while the enemy tires himself*

I want to defeat my opponent without great effort.

> Stratagem 19
>
> *Use silence in order to make noise*

I can never win this battle on my own.

> Stratagem 65
>
> *Lure the bird into the cage*

Success

I want to be successful.

Stratagem 1

A good horse runs by itself

However much I try I have no success.

Stratagem 73

Reach the city of the emperor from the four
celestial directions

I want to make my success last.

Stratagem 95

Do not let the cook work as a tailor

Teamwork

In our team I am the weakest link.

> Stratagem 94
> *Break the mould*

I am part of a team but do my work badly.

> Stratagem 84
> *Play in an orchestra on a broken flute*

Teamwork does not fulfil me.

> Stratagem 100
> *Join the choir*

Timing

I need to time my undertaking correctly.

Stratagem 22

The condition of the road is tested with a single stone

I have missed my chance.

Stratagem 20

Cause distraction by staging a great drama

I am forced to act even though the time is not right.

Stratagem 7

The fox borrows the strength of a tiger

TORMENT

I HAVE to torment others to reach my goal.

STRATAGEM 46
Defend your actions

OTHERS torment me so that they can bring their plans to fulfilment.

STRATAGEM 43
Do not submit under torture

THEY do not see that they torment me.

STRATAGEM 69
Point at the mulberry and criticize the acacia

TRAINING

I AM not trained for the sort of work I would like.

STRATAGEM 35
Trust the growing tree

I WANT to provide my child with the right training.

STRATAGEM 2
Hard polishing makes things shine

MY CHILDREN want to decide for themselves what they will become.

STRATAGEM 91
Learn from the teacher and the tinker

Unity hides division.

TRUST

I TRUST strangers too easily.

STRATAGEM 74

Listen to the nightingale and the rook

MEETING people only with mistrust will not make me happy.

STRATAGEM 66

Never look for a bone in an egg

I HAVE been entrusted with a task that I cannot perform.

STRATAGEM 106

Enter the hut three times

TRUTH

I CANNOT bear the truth.

STRATAGEM 21

Gold does not fear the fire

I WOULD not know the truth if it bit me.

STRATAGEM 2

Hard polishing makes things shine

SOMEONE knows the truth but will not tell me.

STRATAGEM 55

Slaughter the chicken to frighten the monkey

UNDERSTANDING

I AM always full of understanding for others but nobody notices it.

> STRATAGEM 96
>
> *Do not let the wolf be a shepherd*

No one understands my needs, though I am always supposed to be understanding of others.

> STRATAGEM 27
>
> *Offer food only to the hungry*

I WANT to reach a deeper understanding with my partner.

> STRATAGEM 108
>
> *Never mix wine with milk*

Vanity

I want to overcome my vanity.

> Stratagem 21
> *Gold does not fear the fire*

I want to help my partner give up vanity.

> Stratagem 66
> *Never look for a bone in an egg*

I know I am not vain but am accused of vanity.

> Stratagem 33
> *Breathe out the old, breathe in the new*

Victims

I am looking for a suitable victim.

Stratagem 65
Lure the bird into the cage

I have become a victim myself.

Stratagem 42
See the invisible trap

I have become a victim but get no compensation.

Stratagem 17
Steal a beam and replace a post with mouldy wood

Wealth

I have lost the wealth for which I worked hard.

Stratagem 23

Borrow a strange coat in order to make a new beginning

I am a slave to my wealth.

Stratagem 33

Breathe out the old, breathe in the new

I want to use my wealth for something worthwhile.

Stratagem 27

Offer food only to the hungry

Make your abilities your own.

Will

---

I am being forced to do something against
my will.

Stratagem 19

Use silence in order to make noise

I know exactly what I want but cannot find the
opportunity to score a success.

Stratagem 24

Let a water buffalo pull the plough

I am always subject to the will of others.

Stratagem 34

Run away when you have to

WINNING

SOMEONE is disputing my victory.

STRATAGEM 55

Slaughter the chicken to frighten the monkey

I WANT to secure my partner's victory.

STRATAGEM 41

Do not spoil the dogs

I HAVE lost my victory but want to regain it.

STRATAGEM 23

Borrow a strange coat in order to make a new beginning

WAYS TO LIFE MASTERY

WISHES

I HAVE too many wishes all at once.

STRATAGEM 29
Hunt a sheep like a tiger

I AM unable to fulfil my desires.

STRATAGEM 24
Let a water buffalo pull the plough

I AM unable to carry out the wishes of others.

STRATAGEM 27
Offer food only to the hungry

Work

For a long time I have been unemployed and
I want to change the situation.

Stratagem 9

When you have reached the shore, sink the boat

I have not got my work finished and fear the
consequences.

Stratagem 5

Never show the right what is being hidden by the left

I do not like my work but I do not know what
to do about it.

Stratagem 22

The condition of the road is tested with a single stone

World

Weariness

A member of my family has had enough of life.

Stratagem 15

Make noise in the east to attack in the west

One of my friends wants to take his own life.

Stratagem 27

Offer food only to the hungry

I find no joy in life.

Stratagem 13

Fly like a dragon with the wind

YOUTH

WHENEVER I am confronted with youth I become conscious of my age.

STRATAGEM 13

Fly like the dragon with the wind

I WANT to use youth to my advantage.

STRATAGEM 65

Lure the bird into the cage

I WOULD like to mix with young people but they will not accept me.

STRATAGEM 93

Build a fence of wood and bamboo

Everything reaches its goal.